Contents

Going for gold

The Olympics is the greatest sporting show on Earth. Every four years in summer, thousands of competitors known as Olympians flock to one city. There, they compete against the very best in their sport, hoping to win a highly-prized Olympic gold, silver or bronze medal.

Tajikistan's Yusup Abdusalomov (in red) tries to throw Revazi Mindorashvili of Georgia during an Olympic freestyle wrestling bout. Mindorashvili won a gold medal.

ANCIENT OLYMPICS

The ancient Greeks held games at Olympia from 776 BCE for more than a thousand years. At first they competed only in running events, but from 708 BCE wrestling matches were included and later a form of boxing. Ancient Greek boxers could hit opponents when they were on the floor and wore leather thongs called *himantes* around their hands instead of gloves.

Super Star

Hungarian fencer Aladar Gerevich won more gold medals than any other combat contestant at an Olympics. He won a staggering seven gold medals between 1932 and 1960.

OLYMPIC SPORTS

COMBAT SPORTS

Clive Gifford

W
FRANKLIN WATTS
LONDON•SYDNEY

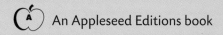 An Appleseed Editions book

Paperback edition 2012

First published in 2011 by Franklin Watts
338 Euston Road, London NW1 3BH

Franklin Watts Australia
Hachette Children's Books
Level 17/207 Kent St, Sydney, NSW 2000

© 2011 Appleseed Editions

Created by Appleseed Editions Ltd,
Well House, Friars Hill, Guestling,
East Sussex TN35 4ET

Designed by Helen James
Edited by Mary-Jane Wilkins
Picture research by Su Alexander

ISBN 978-1-4451-1393-7

Dewey Classification 796.8

A CIP catalogue for this book is available from the British Library.

Picture credits
page 4 Sports Illustrated/Getty Images; 5, 6 & 7 AFP/Getty Images; 8 Getty Images; 9t Joyfull/Shutterstock, b AFP/Getty Images; 10t Pete Niesen/Shutterstock, b Getty Images; 11, 12, & 13 AFP/Getty Images; 14 & 15t Adam Fraise/Shutterstock, 15b AFP/Getty Images; 16 Sports Illustrated/Getty Images; 17t Muzsy/Shutterstock, b Getty Images; 18 Sports Illustrated/Getty Images; 19 & 20 Getty Images; 21, 22, 23 & 24 AFP/Getty Images; 25 Jonathan Larsen/Shutterstock; 26t AFP/Getty Images, b Ian Holmes/Shutterstock; 27, 28 & 29t Getty Images, 29b Diego Barbieri/Shutterstock
Front cover: AFP/Getty Images

Printed in Singapore

Franklin Watts is a division of Hachette Children's Books, an Hachette UK company.
www.hachette.co.uk

MODERN GAMES

The games were revived when the first modern Olympic Games took place in the Greek city of Athens in 1896. Competitors wrestled and fenced at the first modern Olympics, and other combat sports such as boxing, judo and taekwondo were introduced at later games. Today, the host city and nation welcome tens of thousands of spectators, while hundreds of millions more watch on television.

Olympic ooPs

A brutal mix of boxing and wrestling called pankration was first held at the ancient Greek Olympics in 648 BCE. A competitor called Sostratos of Sicyon had a reputation for breaking his opponent's fingers until he surrendered!

FEATS AND RECORDS

The first woman to win an Olympic wrestling gold medal was Irini Merleni from the Ukraine in 2004.

ONE-ON-ONE

Many sports grew up as a result of soldiers training and practising warfare skills, from archery and javelin throwing to fencing, boxing and wrestling. All combat sports at the Olympics pit two opponents against each other in one-on-one competition. For a long time these competitors were men, but in recent games female wrestlers have competed and in 2012, female boxers will take part for the first time.

The 2008 Olympic light heavyweight boxing competition medal winners. China's Xiaoping Zhang (second left) won gold, Ireland's Kenny Egan (left) won silver, and Tony Jeffries and Yerkebulan Shynaliyev both took bronze medals.

Boxing

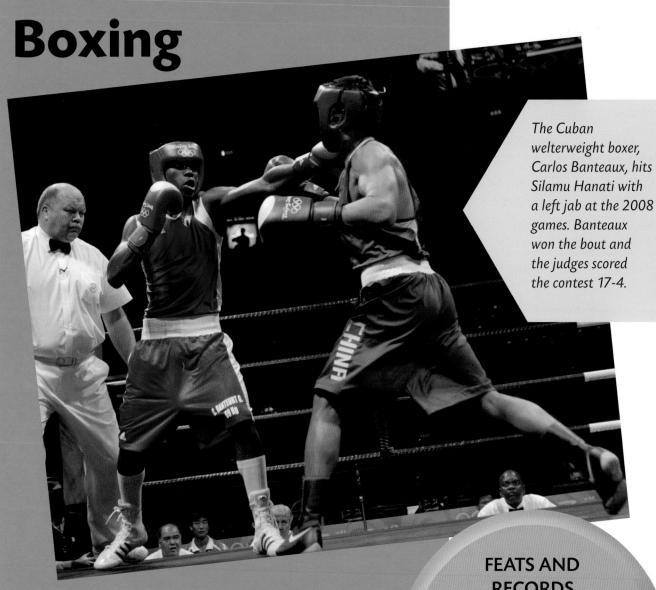

The Cuban welterweight boxer, Carlos Banteaux, hits Silamu Hanati with a left jab at the 2008 games. Banteaux won the bout and the judges scored the contest 17-4.

Boxing has been a popular sport at the Olympics since 1904. In 1912 the games were held in Stockholm and Swedish laws prevented boxers from competing. Since then the best **amateur** boxers in the world have competed against each other at every Olympics.

FEATS AND RECORDS

At the 1984 games in Los Angeles, the USA became the first country to win nine boxing gold medals in a single Olympics. Eight years earlier, brothers Michael and Leon Spinks both won gold medals for the USA.

QUALIFYING FOR THE OLYMPICS

Boxers qualify by winning major amateur championships around the world. They compete in separate competitions depending on their weight. There are 11 weight divisions for men's Olympic boxing, ranging from light flyweight (for boxers under 48 kilos) to super heavyweights weighing more than 91 kilos. Countries send one boxer per weight division.

BOXING BOUTS

At the Olympics, the organizers draw out boxers' names at random, pairing each one with an opponent from the same division. The boxers then fight in **bouts**. As the draw is random the two favourites for a gold medal could meet in the first **round**. Each bout lasts eight minutes and is split into four rounds. The winner progresses to the next match. Eventually two boxers are left to fight in the final for the gold and silver medals. The two losing semi-finalists both receive a bronze medal.

CLOTHING AND PROTECTION

Boxers wear a singlet and shorts in red or blue and padded boxing gloves provided by the Olympic organizers. Boxing is a tough sport and amateur boxers wear a padded head and cheek protector called a headguard, a mouthguard to protect their teeth and a **groin protector** inside their shorts.

RING AND CORNERS

The action takes place inside a 6.1 metre square ring with four ropes tied to corner posts. The floor is made of canvas stretched over a soft underlay which slightly cushions a boxer's fall. Boxers each have a corner to which they return to rest for one minute between rounds. There, the coach gives them water and advice about the next round.

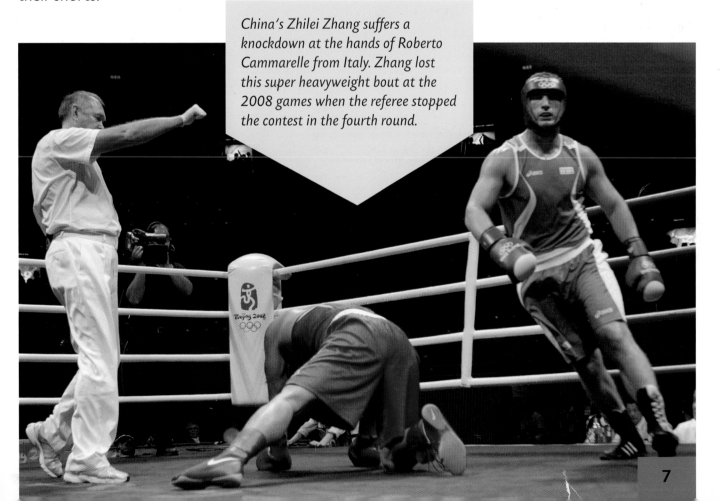

China's Zhilei Zhang suffers a knockdown at the hands of Roberto Cammarelle from Italy. Zhang lost this super heavyweight bout at the 2008 games when the referee stopped the contest in the fourth round.

The referee raises the arm of British boxer James DeGale, winner of the 2008 Olympic middleweight boxing title. DeGale beat Cuban Emilio Correa 16-14 in a close match.

PUNCHING POINTS

Boxers aim to use a range of different punches including **jabs**, crosses and **uppercuts** aimed at an opponent's head and body to wear them out and to score points. Boxers score points when a punch connects firmly with a **scoring area**; these are the central part of the body or the head. The punch must have the weight of the boxer's shoulder or body behind it to score. The boxer must also punch with the part of the glove covering his knuckles.

FEATS AND RECORDS

Cuba's powerful and skilful heavyweight, Teofilo Stevenson, was the first boxer to win three Olympic gold medals in one weight class (1972-1980). He stayed an amateur and retired in 1986.

JUDGES

Five judges sit beside the ring (ringside) and press a scoring button when they believe a punch worth a point has been thrown. When three of the five judges press the button at the same time, a point is awarded. A boxer who scores 20 points more than an opponent automatically wins the bout.

KNOCKDOWNS

A single punch or several blows in a row can lead to a **knockdown**, when a boxer is struck and the hands or body hit the floor of the ring. The referee counts eight seconds and then decides whether the boxer is fit to continue. A boxer who isn't standing after a **count** of ten seconds is knocked out and loses the fight.

George Ungiadze from Georgia puts up his guard against Valeriy Brazhnyk of the Ukraine. Ungiadze's elbows are tucked in, protecting him against a body shot.

A good guard formed by the boxer's arms with the hands held high often helps to **parry** a blow and stop punches reaching their target.

ATTACK AND DEFENCE

Amateur boxers at the Olympics use carefully judged attack and defence moves, but professional boxing puts more emphasis on knocking down an opponent. Boxers use fast footwork and quick reactions to try to stop an opponent scoring, swaying out of range of punches before darting in to score with a blow.

BOXING IN BEIJING

At the 2008 Olympics 11 gold medals went to boxers from nine different countries. Mongolia, the Dominican Republic and China all won their first-ever boxing golds. Boxers from more countries than ever competed, proving that the sport has global appeal today, and Armenia, India and Mauritius all won their country's first boxing medals.

France's Daouda Sow sways out of reach of a punch thrown by Yordenis Ugás of Cuba. Sow defeated Ugás on his way to winning a silver medal in the 2008 games.

When a flurry of punches is thrown by both fighters, the judges wait for a break and then award a point to the fighter they felt had the upper hand.

Olympic OoPs

During the 1964 Olympic games, Valentin Loren of Spain was disqualified for illegal punches against his opponent. Outraged, he attacked the referee, hitting him with a left jab. Loren was banned for life.

EARLY END

A fight can end when one boxer is knocked out or **disqualified**, or in other ways. It stops automatically if one boxer is knocked down and takes a count from the referee three times

FOULS

The referee stands in the ring with the boxers. He looks after the safety of the boxers, orders them to **break** apart if they clutch each other and rules on fouls. These include pushing an opponent, hitting an opponent below the **belt**, in the groin or back of the head, or holding on to an opponent's arms. The referee can warn a boxer who fouls. Three warnings result in disqualification, which means losing the bout.

The referee checks on Gabor Bognar of Hungary during a 2007 bout against Russia's Likhman Vadim. The boxers tested out the Beijing venue before the Olympics the following year.

Super Star

Hungary's Laszlo Papp was the first boxer to win three Olympic gold medals in the middleweight and light-middleweight divisions. He later managed Hungary's national boxing team for 21 years.

Ireland's Katie Taylor (in red) battles with the Ukraine's Yana Zavyalova during the 2007 European Amateur Boxing Championships. Taylor has won this competition five times.

in one round or four times altogether. If one boxer is overwhelmed by an opponent, the referee can step in to stop the bout. There is a doctor at every Olympic fight who can order the bout to be stopped to prevent injury.

TURNING PROFESSIONAL

Success at the Olympics often brings amateur boxers a flood of offers from boxing managers and promoters, who encourage boxers to turn **professional**. Some boxers, such as Muhammad Ali (see page 29), Wladimir Klitschko, the 1968 Olympic heavyweight gold medallist George Foreman, and the 1976 middleweight Olympic champion Sugar Ray Leonard, enjoy global fame and success. Others find professional championship fights tough because they are fought over ten three-minute rounds and protective headgear is not allowed. Despite this, many modern Olympic medallists have turned professional, including British medallists Amir Khan and James DeGale.

FEMALE FIGHTERS

Women's boxing has been growing in popularity and in 2001 the first women's amateur world championships were held in Scranton, USA. The 2012 Olympics will be the first to feature women's boxing. Female boxers will fight in one of three weight divisions: flyweight (48-51 kilos), lightweight (56-60 kilos) and middleweight (69-75 kilos).

Olympic OoPs

At the 1936 Olympics, South Africa's Thomas Hamilton-Brown lost narrowly to Chile's Carlos Lillo. Two days afterwards, a judging error was spotted. Hamilton-Brown was awarded a win, but he had eaten so much in the two days since he'd lost the bout that he had become too heavy to compete in the lightweight division.

Judo

Japan's Ryoko Tamura (left) grapples with Frederique Jossinet of France. They wear loose-fitting judo uniforms called judogi.

Judo is a combat sport in which two competitors called **judoka** grapple with each other. Each tries to unbalance the other so they can perform a sudden and powerful throw or to trap them in a pin, hold or lock which scores points.

Women's judo was demonstrated at the 1988 games and became a full medal sport four years later.

SELF DEFENCE
People of all ages learn and practise judo as a form of unarmed self-defence. The London 2012 Olympics Committee claims that judo

SPORTING HISTORY
Jigoro Kano founded the first judo club, called Kodokan Judo, in Tokyo, Japan, in 1882. Kano became a member of the International Olympic Committee (IOC) in 1909 and tried to persuade the committee to include judo in the games. In 1964 men's judo became the first martial art from Asia to become an Olympic sport.

Super Star

Tadahiro Nomura is the only judoka to win three gold medals. His third gold in a row at the 2004 games was Japan's 100th Olympic gold medal.

is the most popular martial art in the world; 13 million judo students learn it in more than 110 countries.

WEIGHTS AND TIMES

At the Olympics, there are seven weight categories for men and seven for women, ranging from extra lightweight (under 60 kilos for men and under 48 kilos for women) up to the open division for male judoka weighing more than 100 kilos and female judoka over 78 kilos. Bouts last five minutes for men and four minutes for women. When the referee interrupts a bout or instructs the judoka to break, by calling 'matte', the clock is stopped until the judoka separate and move away from each other.

A JUDO BOUT

Contestants compete on a collection of 14-metre-square mats known as tatami. The central eight square metres is the contest area where the action occurs under the watchful eye of a referee. Judoka grip each other's clothing as they try to gain a strong position in which to perform an explosive throw, or use the momentum of their opponent to unbalance them and get them on the floor.

FEATS AND RECORDS

Dutchman Anton Geesink was the first non-Japanese judoka to win a major judo contest. He won a gold medal at the 1964 Olympics, defeating Akio Kaminaga in front of Kaminaga's home crowd.

Kim Jae-Bum of South Korea explodes with delight on winning his bout against Uzbekistan's Shokir Muminov. Kim threw down Muminov to record a winning ippon score.

Leandro Cunha of Brazil tries to get Britain's Colin Oates into a firm hold on the mat at the 2009 Judo World Cup, held in Birmingham.

A PERFECT THROW

The aim of a judoka is to score an **ippon** with a perfect throw of an opponent, landing them on their back with speed and control. A judoka can also score an ippon by demonstrating a hold which pins the opponent on the mat for more than 25 seconds, or if the other judoka submits.

Olympic OoPs

Jung Bu-Kyung reached the final of the men's extra lightweight judo at the 2000 Olympics. Unfortunately, he lasted just 14 seconds before his opponent, Tadahiro Nomura, scored ippon with a perfect throw!

A judoka submits by tapping the mat twice with a hand or by saying, 'maitta' (I submit).

WINNING OR LOSING

If one judoka scores an ippon they win the bout. If neither scores an ippon during a bout, the winner is the judoka with the most points at the end. If the scores are level, the bout continues and the first judoka to score another point becomes the winner. A referee can award penalty points, for example, for foul play or for inactivity – making no attempt to attack an opponent.

SCORING POINTS

There are three other types of point a judoka can score in a judo bout. A waza-ari is scored when a throw or hold is performed well but not quite to ippon standard. If one judoka manages to score two waza-ari in a bout,

British judoka Nathon Burns tries to throw Sofiane Milous of France. A throw which earns a wazi-ari score may be enough to win a close contest.

they win that bout. A judoka scores a yuko when the move isn't good enough to score waza-ari, and the koka is the lowest score of all.

ON THE MAT

Judoka often score points when both opponents are on the mat and no longer standing. One judoka may try to pin an opponent on their back and hold them there. If they can do this well for more than ten seconds, the referee awards points.

China's Xiuli Yang waves to the crowd on the podium at the 2008 games after defeating Cuba's Yalennis Castillo (left) in the final of the 78 kg judo category.

Super Star

France's David Douillet won the men's heavyweight gold in 1996, but suffered a terrible motorcycle accident just a month after. Doctors doubted that he would compete again, but Douillet triumphed in 2000 to win his second gold medal, beating Japan's Shinichi Shinohara.

Wrestling

Wrestling is one of the world's oldest sports and is contested in dozens of different forms around the world. Two forms of wrestling are contested at the Olympics, freestyle and Greco-Roman wrestling. Both test competitors' strength and skill.

Nataliya Synyshyn from the Ukraine lifts and throws Marcie van Dusen of the USA during the 2008 women's 55 kg competition in Beijing. The American wrestler won the bout and finished ninth.

TWO DIFFERENT STYLES

Greco-Roman wrestling developed from wrestling bouts in ancient Greece and Rome. Wrestlers are not allowed to use their legs in holds, and only holds above the hips are permitted. Freestyle wrestlers can hold and grapple their opponent above and below the waist, as well as using their legs to push and lift during a bout.

WRESTLING BOUTS

Wrestlers compete on padded mats inside a nine-metre circle which has a one-metre-wide outer band called the **passivity zone**. Bouts are made up of three rounds, each lasting two minutes. Contestants win points for a range of holds and throws and the highest-scoring wrestler wins the round. The first wrestler to win two rounds wins the bout. Wrestlers aim to pin an opponent to the wrestling mat by the shoulders for a controlled period of time. This move is called a fall and wins them the contest outright.

GRIPPING STUFF

A bout often starts with both wrestlers trying to get a grip on part of their opponent. Grips or holds with the hands that allow a wrestler

Takedowns can be spectacular as both wrestlers hurtle towards the mat. These wrestlers are competing in the the Hungarian Greco-Roman wrestling student Olympics.

to move an opponent around are called **tie-ups**. In a double wrist tie-up, one wrestler firmly grips the opponent's wrists and unbalances them by moving to the side and forcing the opponent's arms down. A wrestler might also attempt a headlock, wrapping an arm around an opponent's neck and locking both their hands together.

Super Star

At the 1896 Olympics, German athlete Carl Schuhmann won the heavyweight Greco-Roman wrestling gold medal. Schuhmann also won three gymnastics gold medals at the games and, amazingly, took part in the weightlifting, long jump, shot-put and triple jump competitions as well.

Agnieszka Wieszczek of Poland (right) wins a bronze medal while Spain's Maider Unda lies on the mat after their bout in the women's freestyle 72 kg category. The red ring is the passivity zone.

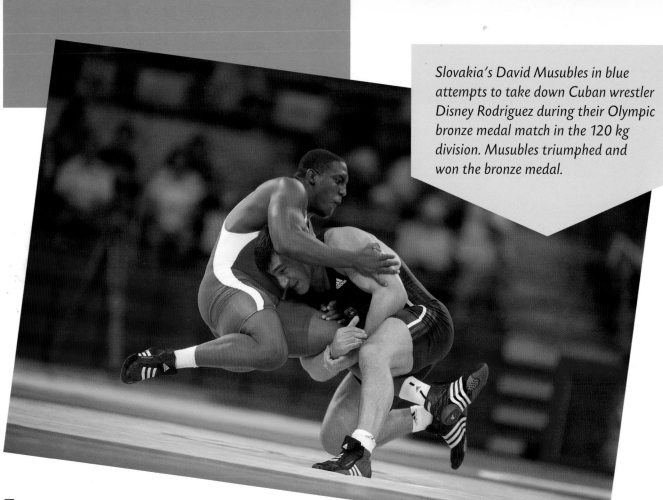

Slovakia's David Musubles in blue attempts to take down Cuban wrestler Disney Rodriguez during their Olympic bronze medal match in the 120 kg division. Musubles triumphed and won the bronze medal.

TAKEDOWNS

In a takedown one wrestler gets the other down on the mat. In both Greco-Roman and freestyle wrestling **takedowns** are worth one, three or five points depending on the quality of the move and how the thrown wrestler lands on the mat. In freestyle competition, wrestlers may try to perform a single leg takedown, by grabbing an opponent's leg, lifting and turning it sharply to force the opponent to lose their balance and fall.

WEIGHT CLASSES

At the Olympics, male wrestlers compete in seven different weight classes in each form of wrestling. Many wrestlers have long careers, during which they move up or down weight divisions. The Hungarian Gyula Bobis started out during the 1920s as a flyweight wrestler, but by 1948, when he finally won an Olympic gold medal, he was a heavyweight.

FEATS AND RECORDS

Swedish wrestlers had a memorable 1932 Olympics. Carl Westergren became the first Greco-Roman wrestler to win three Olympic gold medals (1920, 1924 and 1932). His teammate, Ivar Johansson, unusually won a gold medal in both the Greco-Roman and the freestyle wrestling competitions.

MEDAL BOUTS

Wrestlers in each weight division are divided into pools. The best in each pool contest bouts from which the loser is eliminated, until the final pair of wrestlers compete for the gold and silver medals. Wrestlers beaten by the two finalists enter a separate competition called the repechage. The top two wrestlers in this event are both awarded bronze medals.

WRESTLING WOMEN

Wrestling contests for women were first held at the Olympics in 2004, with four weight divisions for freestyle wrestlers and no Greco-Roman competition. Two of the gold medals went to the Japanese wrestlers Saori Yoshida and Kaori Icho, who repeated their feats by winning again at the 2008 games.

Japan's Kaori Icho (in blue) tries to get a grip on Russia's Alena Kartashova. The Japanese wrestler won gold in the 63 kg category at the 2008 Olympics.

Taekwondo

Taekwondo is an exciting and sometimes spectacular martial art from Korea. The sport is now hugely popular in amateur clubs all over the world and it has been an Olympic sport since 2000.

Spain's Andrea Rica Taboada (left) sways away from a kick by South Korea's Sujeon Lim. The two wear padded body protectors called hogu.

COMPETITION CLOTHING

Taekwondo contestants wear white trousers and a loose fitting jacket tied with a belt. The whole uniform is called a *dobok*. During competitions, contestants wear padded helmets and mouthguards. The body is wrapped in a padded chest protector called a *hogu*. Shinguards protect the front of the legs and contestants also wear forearm guards.

CONTEST AREA

Taekwondo contests take place inside a square matted area called the contest area, surrounded by a border called the competition area. In 2009 the contest area was reduced to eight metres square (from the original ten metres square). Each bout lasts three rounds of three minutes for men and two minutes for women.

FEATS AND RECORDS

Afghanistan attended 12 Olympics without winning a medal until 2008, when Rohullah Nikpai won a bronze in the men's taekwondo 58 kg division. Thousands of Afghans greeted him on his return home.

THE AIM OF THE GAME

Taekwondo is known as the way of the foot and fist. Unlike wrestling or judo, it does not involve grappling, holds, forcing or throwing an opponent on to the mat. Instead, two opponents compete by trying to land accurate, powerful kicks and hand strikes on their opponents.

POINT SCORING

Judges sit at each corner of the competition area. They decide whether a strike is forceful and accurate enough to win points. A kick or blow must strike a scoring area (the padded helmet or trunk protector). One point is awarded for a body hit, two points for a back kick to the body and three points for a successful kick to the head. If scores are equal after three rounds in a final, opponents fight a fourth (sudden death) round to decide the winner.

Cha Dong-Min of South Korea performs a well-timed arm block. He stops his opponent, Akmal Irgashev of Uzbekistan, scoring a point with a high kick to the head. Dong-Min went on to win gold in the over 80 kg class.

21

The gold medallist in the up to 67 kg class, Hwang Kyungseon of South Korea (second left), is joined on the podium by the two bronze medallists and the silver medallist, Karine Sergerie of Canada (left) at the 2008 Olympics.

FAST ATTACKS

Top taekwondo competitors need fast reactions to launch effective attacks on their opponents. They also need flexible bodies so they can twist and turn and aim high kicks at their opponent's head. Competitors often try to attack in combinations – more than one strike in a row – hoping to unbalance their opponent and score points with at least one of the blows.

Super Star

All but one of the USA's taekwondo Olympic medals have been won by a single family! Steven Lopez won two taekwondo gold medals in 2000 and 2004. At the 2008 Olympics, he won bronze while his sister Diana also won bronze and brother Mark won a silver.

SOUND DEFENCE

Contestants try to prevent an opponent's blows from reaching their target. To defend themselves they need to be light and bouncy on their feet, have good balance and be able to move quickly in any direction. Sometimes, contestants use defensive techniques called blocks. These use a hand, arm or leg to **deflect** (turn away) an opponent's kick from a target to stop the opponent scoring points.

PENALTIES

Penalties are awarded for offences or for breaking the rules. A contestant can lose a half point or be given a warning for kyong-go penalties. These include pretending to be hurt, attacking below the waist or grabbing an opponent. Contestants lose a full point for penalties called gam-jeom, which include offences such as throwing an opponent or attacking someone who has fallen to the ground.

WEIGHT DIVISIONS

Contestants compete for eight taekwondo gold medals at each Olympics: four for men and four for women. The different weight divisions are: flyweight (for men under 58 kg and women under 49 kg), featherweight, welterweight and heavyweight (for men over 80 kg and women over 67 kg).

RULE CHANGES

Until the 2008 Olympics, a competitor who won 12 points or was seven points ahead of an opponent won a bout, which ended immediately. These rules were changed by the World Taekwondo Federation in 2009 to encourage competitors to attack more and use more difficult kicks.

FEATS AND RECORDS

Sarah Stevenson won Britain's first Olympic taekwondo medal in 2008, taking a bronze in the heavyweight competition.

Costa Rica's Rafael Castro leaps to make a spectacular attack on Abner Sanchez from El Salvador. The two compete in the men's flyweight (up to 58 kg) class – the lightest division.

Fencing

Fencing grew out of soldiers' sword practice. It is one of just five sports (cycling, gymnastics, athletics and swimming) which have appeared at every modern Olympic games. There are a range of different competitions for both teams and individuals.

China's Xue Tan lunges towards Olena Khomrova of the Ukraine during the 2008 Olympics gold medal match in the women's team sabre competition. The Ukrainian won a very close match by 45 points to 44.

THREE WEAPONS

Fencers compete with one of three weapons at the Olympics – the foil, the sabre or the épée. The foil is the lightest weapon. It is very flexible and only the tip can score a hit, which must be on an opponent's torso, not the legs or arms. The épée is heavier and a hit anywhere on an opponent's body scores. The sabre is a lightweight cutting and thrusting weapon. A hit anywhere above an opponent's waist scores, unless it is on the hands or the back of the head.

Super Star

Nedo Nadi of Italy was only 18 years old when he won a gold medal in the men's foil at the 1912 Olympics. At the 1920 games, he became the only fencer to win gold medals using all three weapons.

FENCING EQUIPMENT

Fencers fight on a 14-metre-long area known as a piste. They wear helmets with visors to protect their faces and a manchette – a protective glove on the hand holding the sword. Each fencer is wired to an electronic scoring system which detects strikes to their electrical body suit (called a lame). A fencing bout lasts for three minutes or until one fencer makes 15 hits.

AGILE ATHLETES

Fencers face each other in the en garde position at the start of a bout with one foot in front of the other and the hand holding the weapon held in front. The other hand curves above the fencer's shoulder. Each fencer tries to attack with speed and cunning, moving into the opponent's range to try to score a hit. In the lunge a fencer thrusts the front leg and sword arm forward in a lightning-fast movement. To make a flèche move the fencer runs forward and thrusts at an opponent as they pass.

Hajnalka Kiarly Picot of France (right) fights Canada's Sherraine MacKay at the 2004 Olympics. Picot's French team were too strong for the Canadians and won the bronze medal.

FEATS AND RECORDS

French fencers have won more Olympic medals than fencers from any other country. The French total of 115 medals includes 41 golds.

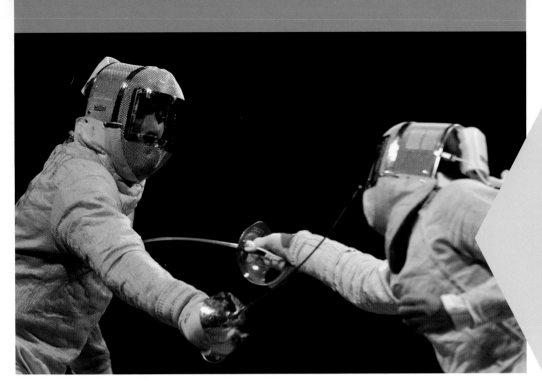

Russia's Stanislav Pozdnyakov (left) tries to parry a thrust from Italy's Giampiero Pastore during the 2008 Olympics team sabre competition. Pozdnyakov has competed in five Olympic Games, winning gold in four.

ATTACK AND DEFENCE

Fencers make thrusts and counter-thrusts. They need to be skilled at defending themselves by parrying, or deflecting, their opponent's weapon away from their bodies. They also need rapid reactions to sway or dodge away from an opponent's weapon. A defending fencer may try to make a **riposte** – a quick thrust following an opponent's attack.

RIGHT OF WAY

Fencers can make a double hit when both strike at almost exactly the same time. Both fencers receive a point when they make double hits in épée bouts. In sabre and foil competitions, there is a right of way rule. Fencers take turns to launch attacks and the turn changes after a fencer has successfully blocked, parried or avoided an attack. If there is a double hit in these bouts only the attacking fencer gains a point.

Andrea Baldini (right) leaps to evade an attack by fellow Italian, Salvatore Sanzo, at a competition in Paris in 2008. Fencers need lightning reactions.

Julien Pillet of France leaps into the air as his country wins the men's team sabre at the 2008 Olympics. The French beat the US 45-37, giving Pillet a second gold to add to the one he won four years earlier.

Super Star

Italian fencer Edoardo Mangiarotti was an extraordinary fencer who competed in Olympics from 1936 to 1960. He won six gold, five silver and two bronze medals, more than any other fencer.

TEAM FENCING

At the Olympics, teams of three fencers take part in the men's and women's team sabre competitions, as well as in the women's foil and men's épée. As the teams compete against each other, the fencers swap every three minutes.

Olympic OoPs

In the 1976 modern pentathlon, Soviet competitor Boris Onischenko was revealed as a cheat. He had a switch added to the grip of his épée which he pressed to register a hit in the electronic scoring system. He was disqualified, although his gold medal from the 1972 games stood.

The judges keep a total of hits made by each team. Competitions last until one team scores 45 hits and wins, or until up to nine fencing bouts have been fought, after which the team with the most points wins.

MODERN PENTATHLON

One other Olympic sport includes fencing. The modern pentathlon is an event in which athletes compete in five different disciplines. It was invented by the founder of the modern Olympics, Baron Pierre de Coubertin. The modern pentathlon was first held for men in 1912 and for women in 2000, when Britain's Stephanie Cook became the first women's gold medallist.

Modern pentathletes score points for their performances in an épée fencing competition, with each bout lasting one minute. The competitors then move on to compete in pistol shooting, a 200-metre freestyle swimming race, a showjumping competition and, finally, a 3,000 metre cross-country run.

Gold medal greats

Combat sports are hugely competitive. Every competitor is intent on victory and achieving a run of victories can be exhausting. The **elite** performers in combat sports reach the Olympics, where some triumph and rise above their rivals. Here are profiles of five of the greats.

ALEKSANDR KARELIN

Russian Aleksandr Karelin is thought to be the greatest Greco-Roman wrestler of all time in the super heavyweight division. No other wrestler has matched his performances. Karelin is an enormously strong athlete, yet quick for his size. He won nine world championships, 11 European championships and three Olympic gold medals (1988, 1992 and 1996) in 13 years of competition during which he didn't lose a contest. His first major loss was at the 2000 Olympic final to American Rulon Gardner.

Olympic OOPs

In his first round bout at the 2008 Olympics, Iran's Hadi Saei fractured his right hand. Hiding the pain and break from opponents, he progressed through the rounds to win the 80 kg gold medal.

HADI SAEI

Iran's most famous martial artist, Hadi Saei is a formidable taekwondo opponent who took up the sport at the age of six. He competed at three Olympics, winning a bronze in 2000 and gold in 2004 in the 68 kg division, before moving up to the 80 kg division to win gold again in 2008.

Aleksandr Karelin (left) battles with American-Iranian Siamak 'Matt' Ghaffari in the 1996 Olympic super heavyweight final. Karelin won the competition without losing a point.

Ryoko Tani is thrown by Algeria's Soraya Haddad during the women's judo 48 kg class quarter final in 2004. Tani won a gold medal.

RYOKO TANI

A judoka standing just 1.46 metres tall is one of the sport's most successful competitors. Ryoko Tani of Japan competed at five Olympics (from 1992 to 2008), winning a medal in each (two golds, two silvers and one bronze) to go with seven world championship gold medals. She is incredibly skilful and during one period in the 1990s won 84 bouts in a row.

VALENTINA VEZZALI

Vezzali is Italy's finest female fencer. She won an Olympic silver in the individual foil and a gold in the team foil at the 1996 Atlanta games. She has won a medal at every Olympics since, becoming the first fencer, male or female, to win three individual foil gold medals in a row (2000, 2004 and 2008).

Valentina Vezzali celebrates another win in the women's foil. As well as seven Olympic medals, Vezzali has won 11 world championship golds.

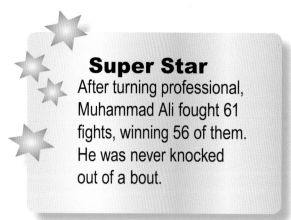

Super Star
After turning professional, Muhammad Ali fought 61 fights, winning 56 of them. He was never knocked out of a bout.

MUHAMMAD ALI

American Muhammad Ali was born Cassius Clay and changed his name in 1964. Ali became famous for his charm, wit and a series of heavyweight world championship boxing fights against the legendary boxers Ken Norton, George Foreman and Joe Frazier. Before he turned professional, he was an outstanding light heavyweight boxer with lightning reactions, who won a gold medal at the 1960 Olympics.

Glossary

amateur   An amateur competes in a sport without being paid.

belt (in boxing)   An imaginary line from the navel to the top of the hips. Boxing opponents may not hit each other below this line.

bout   A contest between two competitors in boxing, judo, wrestling and taekwondo.

break   A referee's order for boxers to step back and separate if they are in a clinch.

count   If a boxer is knocked down, the referee counts to ten seconds. If the boxer is still down, the referee then declares that he has lost the bout by knockout.

deflect   To turn an opponent's arm or leg aside to avoid a blow.

disqualification   To lose a bout for breaking rules or for violent or dangerous conduct.

elite   Top performers in a sport.

groin protector   A padded box or undergarment for men and boys that protects their groin area from blows in boxing and taekwondo.

ippon   The highest score awarded in judo, given for a perfect throw or hold.

jab   A straight, arm-length punch thrown from a boxer's leading hand.

judoka   A person who takes part in judo.

knockdown   A knockdown in boxing and taekwondo happens when one competitor touches the floor with any part of their body other than their feet.

parry   A defensive move in boxing and fencing when the defending competitor pushes and deflects an attack.

passivity zone   A one-metre-wide area on a wrestling mat outside the main competition area.

professional   A professional is paid to perform a sport, especially boxing.

riposte   An attack in fencing launched immediately after the opposing fencer has attacked.

round   One of a series of periods, separated by rests, which make up a boxing bout.

scoring area   The parts of an opponent's head and body in boxing and taekwondo that a competitor strikes to score a point.

takedown   A takedown happens when one wrestler brings an opponent down on to the mat.

tie-up   A grip or hold in wrestling which allows one wrestler to move their opponent around.

uppercut   An upwards-thrown punch designed to hit an opponent's chin.

Books

Inside Sport: Boxing Clive Gifford (Wayland, 2009)
A detailed look at professional and amateur boxing both inside and out of the ring.

Know Your Sport: Judo Paul Mason (Franklin Watts, 2007)
A step-by-step guide to learning judo and competing in bouts.

Olympic Wrestling Barbara M. Linde (Rosen Publishing Group, 2007)
An image-packed guide to some of the great performers and bouts in Olympic wrestling history.

Sporting Skills: Taekwondo Clive Gifford (Franklin Watts, 2010)
A photographic guide to learning key taekwondo techniques.

Fencing for Fun! Suzanne Slade (Compass Point Books, 2008)
An explanation of the sport of fencing for beginners.

Websites

http://www.olympic.org/en/content/Sports/
The official website of the International Olympic Committee (IOC).

http://www.wtf.org/
The homepage of the World Taekwondo Federation.

http://www.fila-wrestling.com/
The official website of FILA, the organization that runs world wrestling.

http://judoinfo.com/new/techniques/animated-throws
A great collection of animations of common judo throws.

http://boxing.about.com/od/amateurs/Amateurs_Olympics.htm
A useful page of links to amateur and Olympic boxing websites.

http://www.talktaekwondo.co.uk/
A website with information on taekwondo techniques and competitions.

Index